BINDING
AND
LOOSING
WALKING IN KINGDOM
AUTHORITY

BINDING AND LOOSING

WALKING IN KINGDOM AUTHORITY

TOM CORNELL

SOZO PUBLISHING

CONTENTS

INTRODUCTION
THE FORGOTTEN KEY

Jesus said something extraordinary to His disciples:

"And I will give you the keys of the kingdom of heaven, and whatever you bind on earth will be bound in heaven, and whatever you loose on earth will be loosed in heaven." (Matthew 16:19 NKJV)

Again, in Matthew 18:18, He repeated the same promise:

"Assuredly, I say to you, whatever you bind on earth will be bound in heaven, and whatever you loose on earth will be loosed in heaven." NKJV

These were not casual words. They were legal, governmental terms — language of authority, not suggestion. Jesus was saying to His sons and daughters:

"You now carry Heaven's keys. You are authorized to permit and

forbid, to open and to shut, to legislate My will on earth as it is in Heaven."

And yet, for many Christians, this revelation has been neglected or misunderstood. We live forgiven but powerless, saved but small, waiting for Heaven someday instead of governing with Christ now. The result is a powerless church, one that endures attack rather than legislating against it, one that often mistakes human conflict for the real spiritual battle.

A Daily Rhythm and a Kingdom Weapon

Binding and loosing is not a spiritual option or a mystical ritual. It is both a daily rhythm of Kingdom life and a weapon for advancing the Kingdom into new territory. As a daily rhythm, binding and loosing is how we steward atmospheres. We bind what Heaven forbids — fear, strife, sickness, deception. We loose what Heaven releases — peace, love, health, truth. It is how we cover our marriages, families, workplaces, and personal lives so that the will of God is consistently enforced.

As a Kingdom advancement weapon, binding and loosing is how we push through resistance when obeying God's call. Just as Moses stood before Pharaoh declaring God's command, "Let My people go," and Pharaoh responded with increased resistance, so it is today. When you take a step to build what God has spoken — to plant a church, launch a business, raise godly children, or break a generational cycle — the enemy stirs opposition. Pharaoh's spirit still resists God's will. In those moments, you need to know how to bind and loose, how to decree and declare, so that Heaven's verdict prevails over the enemy's resistance.

This is not only about protection but about progress. We are not merely survivors in the Kingdom — we are sons and daughters called to build.

The Sons Who Govern

Isaiah prophesied of Jesus:

"For unto us a Child is born, unto us a Son is given; and the government will be upon His shoulder." (Isaiah 9:6, NKJV)

Notice: a Child was born, but a Son was given. A child speaks of birth, but a son speaks of maturity. In Hebrew, the word for son is Ben, which means "the builder of the father's house." Sons are those who carry the responsibility of extending the Father's government. And the government of God rests not on the head, but on the shoulders of the Son — and now, as His body, on the shoulders of the sons and daughters who walk in His name.

This is why Romans 8 tells us creation itself groans, waiting for the revealing of the sons of God (Romans 8:19). The earth is waiting for believers who understand who they are and how to govern.

My Journey Into This Revelation

For a long season of my life, I didn't understand this. I was Spirit-filled, in love with Jesus, passionate to study His Word and share His presence, but I didn't discern the enemy's schemes. When I faced resistance — whether through professors who slandered me in Bible college, or bosses who falsely accused me in the workplace — I only saw people. I thought my battle was with them. I didn't yet know that the enemy was working behind the scenes to discourage me, to tempt me into offense, and to silence my witness. Because I didn't know how to bind and loose, I lived as a victim of the attack instead of a son governing through it.

Later, when doctors declared my wife could never carry children, and when another doctor warned that my newborn son would be handicapped, I began to see differently. Something rose in me. I didn't have a full revelation of binding and loosing yet, but I knew the voice of the Father did not agree with the voice of fear. I learned to reject lies and to stand in faith, and I watched God prove every report wrong. Those moments became prophetic training grounds.

The Call of This Book

This book is written to hand you the same revelation: that you are not merely a Christian waiting for Heaven, but a son or daughter entrusted with the keys of the Kingdom.

- You will see what scripture actually teaches about binding and loosing.
- You will discover your identity as a son who carries the government of God.
- You will learn to live in a daily rhythm of Kingdom authority.
- You will understand how to break through opposition when you advance into new territory.

- You will receive tools, prayers, and decrees to walk this out practically in your family, workplace, ministry, and calling.

By the end of this journey, you will not only understand binding and loosing — you will practice it. You will stand as a priest and king, forbidding what Heaven forbids, releasing what Heaven releases, and advancing the Kingdom of God wherever He has placed you.

The forgotten key is being placed back into your hands. The question is: will you use it?

1

SONS AND THE GOVERNMENT OF GOD

THE PROPHECY OF GOVERNMENT

THE PROPHET ISAIAH DECLARED:

> *"For unto us a Child is born, unto us a Son is given; and the government will be upon His shoulder. And His name will be called Wonderful, Counselor, Mighty God, Everlasting Father, Prince of Peace. Of the increase of His government and peace there will be no end..." (Isaiah 9:6–7, NKJV)*

This prophecy reveals one of the most profound truths of the Kingdom: God's government does not rest in the hands of angels, nor is it carried by abstract spiritual forces — it rests upon the shoulders of the Son. And not just on Jesus as the singular Son of God, but on the mature sons and daughters who are united to Him, who share in His authority, and who extend His rule on the earth.

Isaiah draws a clear distinction: a Child is born, but a Son is given. A child represents birth and potential, but a son represents maturity and responsibility. Sons are trusted with the weight of government. God's Kingdom expands not simply through children of God, but through sons and daughters who understand who they are and who step into their place of authority.

The Meaning of Sonship

In Hebrew, the word for "son" is Ben. It literally means "the builder of the father's house." To be a son is not just to carry a family name — it is to carry a family responsibility. Sons are entrusted to extend, protect, and represent their father's house.

This means that spiritual sonship is not a passive identity; it is an active assignment. To be a son or daughter of God is to be an agent of Heaven's government, a carrier of the Father's authority, and a steward of the Father's will. This explains why creation itself is not groaning for more believers, but for the revealing of the sons of God. Paul writes:

"For the earnest expectation of the creation eagerly waits for the revealing of the sons of God." (Romans 8:19, NKJV)

Creation is waiting for sons who will govern. Waiting for those who will bind what Heaven forbids and loose what Heaven releases. Waiting for those who will enforce the will of God in the earth.

God's Original Design: Dominion

To understand this calling, we have to go back to the beginning. Genesis 1:26–28 gives humanity's original mandate:

"Then God said, 'Let Us make man in Our image, according to Our likeness; let them have dominion... over all the earth...' So God created man in His own image; in the image of God He created him; male and female He created them. Then God blessed them, and God said to them, 'Be fruitful and multiply; fill the earth and subdue it; have dominion...'" NKJV

From the very beginning, humanity was created to reign. Adam and Eve were given dominion, not over each other, but over creation. Their assignment was to extend Eden — the place where Heaven and earth met — until the whole earth was filled with the glory of God.

That word "dominion" in Hebrew carries the sense of rulership, governing, and stewardship. God's design was that His image-bearers would administrate His will in the visible world. Heaven would rule the unseen realm, and humanity would extend that rule into the seen.

This is why Jesus' teaching on binding and loosing is so revolutionary. He was not giving His disciples a new concept; He was restoring the original mandate. Binding and loosing is dominion language. It is sons and daughters administrating the Father's will on the earth.

Priests and Kings

The New Testament confirms this dual role. Revelation 1:6 declares:

"...and has made us kings and priests to His God and Father, to Him be glory and dominion forever and ever. Amen." NKJV

And again in Revelation 5:10:

"And have made us kings and priests to our God; and we shall reign on the earth." NKJV

We are not merely worshippers, though we are called to worship. We are not merely intercessors, though prayer is central. We are also kings — rulers, governors, legislators. Priests minister to God; kings administrate for God. Priests carry presence; kings carry authority. And in Christ, we are both.

This is crucial to understand because many believers embrace their priesthood (ministering to God in worship, prayer, and devotion) but neglect their kingship. We must do both. Sons of God stand in God's presence and then step out with His authority.

The Shoulders of the Body

Isaiah said the government would be upon the shoulders of the Son. Shoulders are part of the body. And Scripture tells us that Christ is the Head, and we are His Body (Colossians 1:18). This means the government of God rests not on Christ alone in Heaven, but on His Body on the earth.

If the Head carries the plan, the Body carries the weight. Sons and daughters are the shoulders that bear the responsibility of governing the Father's house on earth.

This changes everything about how we see Christianity. The gospel is not merely about going to Heaven one day —

it is about Heaven invading earth through sons and daughters today. The Christian life is not passive waiting; it is active governing.

My Early Misunderstanding

When I first came to Christ, I was consumed with His presence. I loved to worship, to study His Word, to tell others about Him. And I was experiencing fruit — people were touched by the glory of God in my life. But when opposition came, I had no grid for it.

I went to a Christian university where professors openly opposed me. One spread lies, accused me falsely, and mocked my passion for the Word. At the time, I thought it was just a difficult personality. I didn't see the spiritual reality behind the attack. I carried offense. I was discouraged. I even wondered if God was distant.

Looking back, I realize I didn't know I was a son carrying the government of Heaven. I didn't know I could bind the spirit of slander and loose truth. I didn't know I could forbid the enemy's schemes and release God's favor. I lived as though I had no authority.

This is why this revelation matters. Without it, we remain victims of circumstance. With it, we rise as sons who govern with Christ.

Creation Is Waiting

Paul's words in Romans 8 come alive here. Creation is waiting for the revealing of the sons of God. The Greek word for "revealing" is apokalypsis — an unveiling. It is the same word used for the Book of Revelation.

The earth is groaning for an unveiling of sons and daughters who know who they are, who recognize their authority, and who take up the keys of the Kingdom. It is waiting for believers who will not only worship in private but legislate in public.

This is why binding and loosing is so central. It is the practical outworking of sonship. It is how we govern atmospheres, steward families, protect marriages, and advance the Kingdom into new territory. It is how we carry the government of God on our shoulders.

A Growing Government

Isaiah didn't just say the government rests on His shoulders. He said:

> *"Of the increase of His government and peace there will be no end." (Isaiah 9:7 NKJV)*

The government of God is not shrinking; it is increasing. The Kingdom is advancing, and it will never stop advancing. But here's the key: that increase happens through us. The expansion of God's government in the earth happens as sons and daughters bind and loose, legislate and decree, forbid and permit.

Every time you bind fear in your home and loose peace, the government increases. Every time you bind sickness and loose healing, the government increases. Every time you bind deception and loose truth, the government increases. The increase of His government has no end because the authority of His sons and daughters has no limit in Him.

Reflection and Activation

Let's pause and reflect.

- Do I see myself as a son or daughter entrusted with the Father's house, or merely as a believer waiting for Heaven?
- Am I actively carrying the government of God into my workplace, my family, my community?
- Do I understand that my words, prayers, and decrees are not suggestions but legislation?

Now, let's activate. Pray this aloud:

Father, thank You that You have made me Your child, but also Your son. Thank You that You have placed Your government on the shoulders of Jesus, and as part of His Body, I share in carrying that government on the earth. I repent for every way I have lived passively, waiting for Heaven instead of releasing Heaven. Today, I take my place as a son. I declare that I am a builder of my Father's house. I bind fear, lies, and discouragement. I loose faith, truth, and courage. I carry Your government into my home, my work, and my community. In Jesus' name, amen.

The foundation of binding and loosing is sonship. Until you see yourself as a son or daughter who carries the government of God, binding and loosing will feel like formulas instead of authority. But when you realize the government rests on your shoulders, everything changes.

You are not merely a believer. You are a son. You are not merely a churchgoer. You are a builder of your Father's house. You are not merely a servant of God. You are a priest and king, carrying His presence and His power.

This is where the journey begins. The keys of the Kingdom belong to sons who understand the weight of government. And as you step into that revelation, you will find that Heaven itself backs your words.

2

THE KEYS OF THE KINGDOM
THE CONVERSATION AT CAESAREA PHILIPPI

ONE OF THE MOST PIVOTAL MOMENTS IN THE GOSPELS happens at Caesarea Philippi. Jesus gathers His disciples and asks them a question that cuts to the heart:

> *"Who do men say that I, the Son of Man, am?" (Matthew 16:13, NKJV)*

The disciples give the rumors of the day: John the Baptist, Elijah, Jeremiah, or another prophet. Then Jesus presses deeper:

> *"But who do you say that I am?" (v. 15).*

Simon Peter answers with boldness and revelation:

> *"You are the Christ, the Son of the living God." (v. 16).*

Jesus responds with a declaration that reverberates through history:

"Blessed are you, Simon Bar-Jonah, for flesh and blood has not revealed this to you, but My Father who is in heaven. And I also say to you that you are Peter, and on this rock I will build My church, and the gates of Hades shall not prevail against it. And I will give you the keys of the kingdom of heaven, and whatever you bind on earth will be bound in heaven, and whatever you loose on earth will be loosed in heaven." (vv. 17–19) NKJV

Here Jesus introduces the keys of the Kingdom. Notice when He gave them: after revelation. Peter saw who Jesus truly was — not by logic, not by tradition, but by revelation from the Father. And revelation unlocked authority. This teaches us an unshakable principle: authority flows from revelation.

What Are Keys?

In the ancient world, keys were large, often carried on the shoulder. They symbolized authority, access, and responsibility. To hold the keys of a house meant you could open and close, admit or forbid, allow or deny. Isaiah 22:22 foreshadowed this concept:

"The key of the house of David I will lay on his shoulder; so he shall open, and no one shall shut; and he shall shut, and no one shall open." NKJV

Keys represent delegated government. They are not ornamental; they are functional. A person with keys has both privilege and duty. When Jesus says, "I give you the keys of the Kingdom of Heaven," He is saying:

"I entrust you with the authority to administrate Heaven's will

on earth. *What you open, Heaven backs. What you close, Heaven enforces."*

Binding and Loosing: Rabbinic Language

To first-century Jewish ears, Jesus' words were not strange. Rabbis used the terms bind and loose to mean forbid and permit. They would "bind" a practice as unlawful, or "loose" a practice as acceptable, based on their interpretation of Torah. Jesus takes this familiar language and gives it to His disciples with Kingdom weight:

"You will forbid what Heaven forbids, and you will permit what Heaven permits."

This is important: binding and loosing is not about personal opinion or preference. It is about alignment. We don't make Heaven agree with us — we agree with Heaven. The keys of the Kingdom do not give us license to legislate our will; they give us authority to legislate God's will.

Two Passages, One Principle

Jesus speaks of binding and loosing in two different contexts.

1. Matthew 16:19 — revelation of Christ and the promise of the keys.

Authority comes from knowing who Jesus is. The Church built on this revelation cannot be overcome by the gates of hell.

2. Matthew 18:18–20 — the context of forgiveness, discipline, and agreement.

Authority is exercised together. Agreement multiplies binding and loosing power. The presence of Jesus is promised when two or three gather in His name.

Together these passages teach us: binding and loosing is both personal (flowing from my revelation of Christ) and corporate (strengthened in agreement with others).

Guardrails of Authority

Genesis 1 reminds us: God gave humanity dominion over fish, birds, animals, and the earth — but not over other humans. We are never called to bind people. Our authority is spiritual, not manipulative. Paul makes this clear in Ephesians 6:12:

"For we do not wrestle against flesh and blood, but against principalities, against powers, against the rulers of the darkness of this age, against spiritual hosts of wickedness in the heavenly places."

This is a crucial guardrail: our battle is with spiritual forces, not people. Binding and loosing is never about controlling a boss, a spouse, or a neighbor. It is about forbidding the demonic forces influencing situations and releasing God's will into them.

Authority Without Revelation

Early in my walk, I didn't understand this. I loved Jesus, but I didn't grasp the authority of the keys. When a professor slandered me in Bible college, I thought the battle was against him. I didn't see the spiritual resistance behind his words.

Because I lacked revelation, I carried offense instead of exercising authority. I endured what I could have forbidden. I suffered under lies I could have bound. I left unspoken truths I could have loosed.

Revelation changes everything. Once you know who Jesus is, you begin to know who you are in Him. And once you know who you are, you stop living under circumstances and start legislating over them.

Heaven's Backing

The Greek wording in Matthew 16:19 is best translated:

"Whatever you bind on earth will have been bound in heaven; whatever you loose on earth will have been loosed in heaven."
NKJV

This makes the picture clearer: we don't initiate Heaven's will — we enforce it. We are enforcers, not inventors. We stand as earthly legislators of heavenly decrees.

When you bind fear, you are echoing Heaven's verdict that fear has no place in Christ's Kingdom (2 Timothy 1:7). When you loose healing, you are echoing Heaven's decree that by His stripes we are healed (Isaiah 53:5). This is why Jesus could say, "Your will be done, on earth as it is in heaven" (Matthew 6:10). Binding and loosing is how we make that prayer tangible.

Keys Open and Shut Doors

Keys are not just symbols of binding and loosing; they are tools for opening and shutting. In Revelation 3:7, Jesus describes Himself as the One who "has the key of David, He who opens and no one shuts, and shuts and no one opens."

When we exercise Kingdom authority, doors open and shut. Opportunities align. Favor is released. Curses are broken. The keys of the Kingdom unlock destiny and lock out darkness.

Have you ever felt like a door was shut in your face when you knew God called you forward? Often that is a moment to pick up the keys — to bind the resistance and to loose the favor of God. Sons and daughters don't stand helpless before closed doors; they legislate in alignment with Heaven until God's purpose prevails.

Practical Application: Using the Keys

So how do we use the keys of the Kingdom?

1. Receive revelation. Authority flows from knowing who Christ is and who you are in Him.
2. Discern Heaven's will. Ask: What does Heaven permit here? What does Heaven forbid?
3. Speak with authority. Binding and loosing happens with words. We legislate with decrees, not thoughts.

4. Stay within guardrails. We forbid demonic influence, not people. We loose God's purposes, not our preferences.
5. Stand in agreement. Whenever possible, bind and loose with others — spouses, family, church. Agreement multiplies impact.

Reflection Questions

- Am I living as one who holds keys, or as one waiting for someone else to open doors for me?
- Do I see binding and loosing as formulas, or as governmental decrees backed by Heaven?
- Have I misdirected my authority toward people instead of the powers influencing them?
- In what area of my life right now do I need to forbid what Heaven forbids and release what Heaven releases?

Activation Prayer

Father, thank You for entrusting me with the keys of the Kingdom. I receive this authority not as my own power, but as delegated authority in Christ. I repent for every time I have lived as if I had no keys, for every time I have fought people instead of principalities, for every time I have agreed with lies instead of enforcing Your truth. Today, I take the keys in my hand. I bind fear, confusion, and opposition in my home, my workplace, and my calling. I loose peace, clarity, and favor in every sphere of influence You have given me. I declare that doors no man can shut are opening before me, and every door of darkness is closed in Jesus' name. Amen.

The keys of the Kingdom are not symbolic ornaments for believers to admire — they are functional tools for sons and daughters to use. With them, we forbid what Heaven forbids, permit what Heaven permits, and open and shut doors in alignment with God's will.

When Jesus placed the keys into the hands of His disciples, He was entrusting them with Heaven's authority. Today, He places them in your hands. The question is no longer, "Do you have the keys?" The question is, "Will you use them?"

3

DAILY AUTHORITY: A LIFESTYLE OF BINDING AND LOOSING

NOT JUST FOR CRISIS, BUT FOR LIFESTYLE

MANY BELIEVERS ONLY THINK OF BINDING AND LOOSING WHEN they face crisis. A spiritual attack comes, a diagnosis arrives, or a conflict erupts — and suddenly they pray, decree, or cry out for deliverance. But Jesus never intended binding and loosing to be used only in emergencies.

He gave the keys of the Kingdom as tools for daily life. They are meant to be the rhythm of every believer's walk with God, not just the weapon of last resort. Just as you wouldn't leave the doors of your home unlocked day after day, you don't leave the doors of your life spiritually unguarded. Sons and daughters use their keys daily.

Authority in Daily Life

Jesus gave His disciples this encouragement after their ministry trip:

"Then the seventy returned with joy, saying, 'Lord, even the demons are subject to us in Your name.' And He said to them, 'I

saw Satan fall like lightning from heaven. Behold, I give you the
authority to trample on serpents and scorpions, and over all the
power of the enemy, and nothing shall by any means hurt you."
(Luke 10:17–19, NKJV)

Notice that Jesus didn't say, "You have authority only when things get really bad." He said, "I give you authority." It is a present-tense gift, a lifestyle reality. Every day, you and I walk in enemy territory. Every day, we encounter thoughts, atmospheres, and situations shaped by darkness. And every day, we are called to enforce Heaven's rule. Paul echoes this in Colossians 3:1–3:

"If then you were raised with Christ, seek those things which are
above, where Christ is, sitting at the right hand of God. Set your
mind on things above, not on things on the earth. For you died,
and your life is hidden with Christ in God." NKJV

Our position is secure: raised with Christ, hidden in Him, seated with Him. But our responsibility is daily: to set our minds on things above, to enforce that heavenly reality in our earthly environment.

Three Spheres of Daily Binding and Loosing

There are at least three practical spheres where binding and loosing must be applied as a daily rhythm.

1. Guarding Your Thought Life

Every day, thoughts come that do not align with Heaven — thoughts of fear, shame, doubt, lust, anger, or despair.

Left unchecked, these thoughts build strongholds. Paul writes:

"For the weapons of our warfare are not carnal but mighty in God for pulling down strongholds, casting down arguments and every high thing that exalts itself against the knowledge of God, bringing every thought into captivity to the obedience of Christ."
(2 Corinthians 10:4–5, NKJV)

This is binding and loosing in the thought life:

- Bind arguments, lies, and imaginations that exalt themselves against God's truth.
- Loose the mind of Christ, peace of God, and truth of Scripture into your thinking.

If you do not bind lies daily, they will accumulate. If you do not loose truth daily, you will drift into defeat.

2. Covering Your Family and Relationships

The enemy seeks to sow discord in marriages, rebellion in children, and strife in households. Paul urges husbands and wives to walk in love and children to walk in obedience (Ephesians 5–6) — because those areas are constant battlefields. Daily binding and loosing for your family might sound like:

- *"I bind every spirit of division, confusion, and strife that seeks to operate in my marriage. I loose unity, love, and covenant blessing over our home."*
- *"I bind rebellion, deception, and premature death over*

my children. I loose destiny, wisdom, and the fear of
the Lord into their lives."

This isn't just crisis management — it's daily spiritual covering.

3. Stewarding Your Workplace and Assignment

Workplaces are not spiritually neutral. They are full of pressures, politics, competition, and compromise. Too many believers separate "church" from "career," forgetting that the Kingdom mandate extends into every sphere. Jesus said:

"You are the salt of the earth... You are the light of the world. A
city that is set on a hill cannot be hidden." (Matthew 5:13–14,
NKJV)

Being salt and light in your workplace requires spiritual stewardship. Every day you can:

- Bind dishonesty, jealousy, and backbiting.
- Loose integrity, excellence, and favor.
- Bind fear of man and intimidation.
- Loose boldness, wisdom, and divine creativity.

You don't need to stand in the middle of the office shouting decrees. But in prayer, in your spirit, and sometimes under your breath, you can govern the atmosphere.

My Experience With Missing the Daily Rhythm

Early in my walk, I didn't know this. When my boss at the cell tower company lied about me to cover his mistakes,

I just absorbed the injustice. I thought the battle was with him. I didn't realize the enemy was exploiting the situation to provoke anger and bitterness in me. Because I wasn't binding offense daily, bitterness took root. Because I wasn't loosing peace and forgiveness daily, I felt weighed down and spiritually drained.

Later, as I learned the principle of daily authority, I realized I could have stopped that scheme. I could have bound the spirit of accusation and loosed the favor of God over my work. Instead of being weighed down, I could have walked in confidence, knowing Heaven was backing me.

Daily Authority Shapes Atmospheres

Think of your daily authority like the thermostat in your home. Without intentional setting, the atmosphere drifts. But when you set the thermostat, the environment aligns with your choice.

Binding and loosing is how you set the thermostat of your life, family, and environment. Left ungoverned, atmospheres drift toward chaos. Governed with authority, atmospheres align with Heaven.

The Lord's Prayer as a Daily Model

Jesus gave us the Lord's Prayer in Matthew 6:9–13, and it is more than a ritual; it is a template for daily authority.

- "Our Father in heaven, hallowed be Your name."
  — Begin with worship and alignment.

- "Your kingdom come. Your will be done on earth as it is in heaven." — Bind what opposes His will, loose what aligns with His will.
- "Give us this day our daily bread." — Loose provision, wisdom, and strength.
- "Forgive us our debts, as we forgive our debtors." — Bind unforgiveness, loose mercy and grace.
- "Do not lead us into temptation, but deliver us from the evil one." — Bind temptation and deception, loose deliverance and protection.

This prayer is the daily rhythm of binding and loosing in action.

Consistency Builds Strength

Authority grows with consistency. A soldier does not wait for war to practice with his weapon; he trains daily. Likewise, believers should not wait for crisis to practice authority. Every day you practice binding and loosing, you sharpen your discernment, strengthen your spirit, and normalize living as a son or daughter governing with Christ. Neglecting daily authority leaves doors open for the enemy. Exercising daily authority builds a habit of victory.

Reflection Questions

1. Am I using the keys of the Kingdom only in crisis, or as part of my daily walk?
2. Do I regularly bind lies and loose truth over my thought life?
3. Have I been passive about covering my marriage, children, or household with spiritual authority?

4. Do I see my workplace as an assignment to steward spiritually, or just as a job to survive?

Activation Prayer

Pray this aloud today as a declaration of daily rhythm:

Father, I thank You that You have given me daily authority in Christ. Today, I set my mind on things above. I bind fear, lies, and every thought that exalts itself against Your truth. I loose the peace of Christ, the wisdom of the Spirit, and the truth of Your Word in my mind. I bind division, strife, and confusion in my marriage and family. I loose unity, love, and blessing over my home. I bind dishonesty, jealousy, and intimidation in my workplace. I loose favor, excellence, and creativity in my assignment. Today, I walk as a son who governs, not a servant who reacts. I choose to set the atmosphere of my life in alignment with Heaven. In Jesus' name, amen.

Binding and loosing is not an occasional tool; it is a daily lifestyle. Sons and daughters carry the government of God on their shoulders, and that government is exercised not just in the dramatic battles, but in the ordinary rhythms of life. When you bind lies and loose truth each day, you walk in peace. When you bind strife and loose love daily, you cultivate unity. When you bind fear and loose boldness daily, you carry courage.

The Christian life is not waiting for Heaven — it is walking with Heaven's keys today.

4

ADVANCING THE KINGDOM: BINDING AND LOOSING IN WARFARE

WHEN OBEDIENCE MEETS RESISTANCE

ONE OF THE MOST MISUNDERSTOOD ASPECTS OF THE Christian life is this: when you step forward to obey God, life doesn't always get easier — sometimes it gets harder. Advancement in the Kingdom almost always provokes opposition. We see this clearly in the story of Moses. God calls him to deliver Israel, and Moses courageously stands before Pharaoh with God's word:

> "Afterward Moses and Aaron went in and told Pharaoh, 'Thus says the Lord God of Israel: "Let My people go, that they may hold a feast to Me in the wilderness."'" (Exodus 5:1, NKJV)

But Pharaoh does not yield. In fact, he makes the Israelites' burden heavier:

> "You shall no longer give the people straw to make brick as before. Let them go and gather straw for themselves. And you shall lay on them the quota of bricks which they made before. You shall not reduce it." (vv. 7–8) NKJV

Moses obeyed, but Pharaoh resisted. God's will was declared, but hell doubled down. This is what often happens when you step into Kingdom assignments — when you plant a church, launch a ministry, start a Kingdom business, or break a generational cycle. Pharaoh's spirit still rises. The enemy resists because he knows territory is being taken.

Advancement Always Provokes Warfare

Paul experienced the same pattern in Acts 16. While ministering in Philippi, a slave girl possessed with a spirit of divination followed Paul and Silas, disrupting their ministry. Paul cast the spirit out in the name of Jesus. Immediately, persecution erupted. Paul and Silas were beaten and thrown in prison. But what happened next? At midnight, they prayed and sang hymns. Heaven shook the prison, the chains fell off, and the jailer and his household were saved. Out of resistance came revival.

This is the principle: advancement provokes warfare, but warfare precedes breakthrough. When you understand this, you stop interpreting opposition as failure. Instead, you recognize it as confirmation that you are advancing. Pharaoh's resistance means you are on the right path. Hell's retaliation means Heaven's purposes are breaking through.

The Role of Binding and Loosing in Advancement

This is where binding and loosing becomes critical. Daily authority guards your life, but advancement authority confronts resistance. When Pharaoh says no, binding and loosing enforces Heaven's yes. When the enemy lies, binding and loosing silences his voice and looses God's truth. When resistance rises, binding and loosing becomes the battering ram of the Kingdom. Jesus promised:

"...I will build My church, and the gates of Hades shall not prevail against it." (Matthew 16:18, NKJV)

Gates are defensive structures. The church is not meant to cower behind walls; we are called to storm the gates. And the keys of the Kingdom are how we do it.

Keys for Times of Resistance

What kinds of situations require advancing authority?

- Planting churches — binding spiritual resistance in a region, loosing revival and hunger for God.
- Launching ministries — binding distraction and division, loosing provision and favor.
- Expanding in business — binding greed, dishonesty, and fear, loosing integrity, excellence, and influence.
- Breaking generational cycles — binding curses of addiction, poverty, and dysfunction, loosing blessing, freedom, and generational destiny.

Advancement is not possible without authority. Sons and daughters cannot take new territory by human effort alone; they must bind what resists and loose what Heaven decrees.

My Family's Testimony: Binding Lies, Loosing Truth

I will never forget when doctors told my wife she could not carry children. The report was final: her womb could not sustain life beyond a certain stage. But something rose up in my spirit. I knew this was not the voice of Heaven.

At the time, I didn't have full language for "binding and loosing," but that's what I was doing. I refused to bind myself to the lie. I refused to loose fear into our future. Instead, I bound the diagnosis in the spirit, and I loosed the truth of God's Word — that He opens and closes the womb, and that His promises override man's impossibilities.

A prophetic word came shortly after, confirming that we would raise both biological and adopted children. And within months, my wife was pregnant with our son. The one the doctors said could not exist came into the world healthy, whole, and strong. Later, another son followed. Today, those children are a living testimony of binding lies and loosing truth in the face of Pharaoh's resistance.

The Pattern of Pharaoh's Spirit

Pharaoh's spirit manifests in many ways today:

- Through systems — unjust laws, corruption, or policies that oppose righteousness.
- Through people — bosses, leaders, or authorities manipulated by spiritual forces.
- Through circumstances — sudden obstacles, delays, or opposition when you step into obedience.

But Pharaoh's pattern is always the same: he increases

pressure to discourage obedience. He makes the "bricks without straw" seem unbearable, hoping you will give up. The key is to recognize that resistance is not a sign to retreat, but a signal to bind and loose.

Biblical Weapons for Advancement

Scripture gives us clear weapons for these moments:

- The Word of God — Jesus resisted Satan in the wilderness with, "It is written..." (Matthew 4:4,7,10). Binding and loosing is always anchored in Scripture.
- The Blood of Jesus — Revelation 12:11 says we overcome by the blood of the Lamb and the word of our testimony. His blood silences every accusation of the enemy.
- The Name of Jesus — Philippians 2:9–10 reminds us that His name is above every name. Binding is done in His authority, not ours.
- Agreement in Prayer — Matthew 18:19–20 emphasizes the multiplying power of agreement. Advancing battles are often won together.

When you combine these weapons with the keys of binding and loosing, resistance crumbles.

Reflection: Resistance as Confirmation

Too often, believers misinterpret resistance. They assume, "If it's hard, maybe I missed God." But biblically, the opposite is often true. Resistance is proof you are advancing. Paul wrote to the Corinthians:

"...for a great and effective door has opened to me, and there are many adversaries." (1 Corinthians 16:9, NKJV)

The presence of adversaries did not mean the door was closed — it meant the door was open. Ask yourself:

- Am I interpreting resistance as a closed door, or as confirmation of an open one?
- Am I binding lies and intimidation, or retreating under pressure?
- Am I loosing God's promises boldly, or shrinking back in fear?

Sample Declarations for Advancement

Here are prayers you can speak in advancing seasons:

- "I bind every spirit of resistance, intimidation, and delay standing against the will of God in my life. I loose acceleration, favor, and breakthrough in Jesus' name."
- "I bind lies, false reports, and discouragement. I loose truth, courage, and divine perspective."
- "I bind the Pharaoh spirit that seeks to enslave and oppress. I loose freedom, deliverance, and the power of God's Word to prevail."

Declarations like these are not positive thinking; they are legislative acts. They are the exercise of keys entrusted to sons and daughters.

Worship as Warfare

Notice in Acts 16, Paul and Silas didn't just bind and loose with words — they sang. Worship was their warfare. At midnight, as they worshiped, Heaven shook the prison. Worship looses Heaven's presence into the darkest places. This is why binding and loosing is never mechanical. It flows from intimacy. When you hear God's voice, when you align with His Word, and when you lift His name in worship, authority flows. Pharaoh cannot resist a worshipping church.

Activation Prayer

Pray this aloud over your assignment:

Father, thank You that You have entrusted me with keys for advancement. Today I choose not to retreat in the face of resistance. Like Moses before Pharaoh, I declare Your Word boldly. Like Paul and Silas in prison, I lift my voice in worship. I bind every spirit of resistance, intimidation, and delay. I loose Your favor, breakthrough, and acceleration. I declare that every assignment You have spoken will prevail, and every Pharaoh spirit will bow to the name of Jesus. I advance not in my own strength, but in the authority of the Kingdom. In Jesus' name, amen.

Advancement in the Kingdom will always provoke resistance. Pharaoh will always say no before Heaven enforces yes. But the keys of the Kingdom were given for such moments. When you bind lies and loose truth, when you stand firm under pressure, when you decree God's promises with boldness, you discover that resistance is only the stage for God's power to be revealed.

You were not called to retreat under pressure. You were called to advance with authority. The gates of hell will not prevail — not against the Church, and not against the son or daughter who wields the keys of the Kingdom.

5

DISCERNING AND RESISTING THE ENEMY

THE THIEF'S AGENDA

Jesus made the enemy's mission unmistakably clear:

"The thief does not come except to steal, and to kill, and to destroy. I have come that they may have life, and that they may have it more abundantly." (John 10:10, NKJV)

The devil never takes a day off. His tactics are consistent: steal joy, kill hope, destroy identity, fracture families, divide churches, derail destinies. If we do not discern his schemes, we can spend years fighting shadows — blaming people, circumstances, or even God — while the true thief robs us unchecked.

Binding and loosing requires spiritual discernment. If you bind the wrong thing, you waste authority. If you fail to bind what Heaven forbids, you allow demonic activity to linger. Sons and daughters must learn to see through the surface and recognize the spiritual reality beneath.

The Armor of God: Standing in Authority

Paul lays out our defense and offense in Ephesians 6:10–18:

> "Finally, my brethren, be strong in the Lord and in the power of His might. Put on the whole armor of God, that you may be able to stand against the wiles of the devil. For we do not wrestle against flesh and blood, but against principalities, against powers, against the rulers of the darkness of this age, against spiritual hosts of wickedness in the heavenly places."

Notice Paul's clarity: we do not wrestle against flesh and blood. People are not the enemy. Behind human conflict are powers and principalities. Binding and loosing is never about manipulating people; it is about confronting the unseen forces influencing them.

The armor of God is both positional and practical:

- Truth (belt) — exposes lies.
- Righteousness (breastplate) — protects the heart.
- Peace (shoes) — stabilizes your steps.
- Faith (shield) — extinguishes fiery darts.
- Salvation (helmet) — guards the mind.
- The Word of God (sword) — strikes offensively.
- Prayer — activates it all.

Binding and loosing flows from standing fully armored. Without discernment and armor, we misfire our authority.

Strongholds and Lies

Paul gives further clarity in 2 Corinthians 10:3–5:

"For though we walk in the flesh, we do not war according to the flesh. For the weapons of our warfare are not carnal but mighty in God for pulling down strongholds, casting down arguments and every high thing that exalts itself against the knowledge of God, bringing every thought into captivity to the obedience of Christ." NKJV

Here we see where battles often begin: strongholds of thought. The enemy plants lies, distortions, or accusations that take root in the mind. Left unchallenged, they become fortresses. Binding and loosing here looks like this:

- Bind lies, arguments, and false imaginations.
- Loose truth, wisdom, and the mind of Christ.

Discernment is key — is the heaviness I feel just a mood, or is it a spirit of heaviness (Isaiah 61:3)? Is the conflict in my workplace just personality, or is there a spirit of strife stirring? Is the fear in my heart just human anxiety, or is it a spirit of fear (2 Timothy 1:7)?

Common Tactics of the Enemy

The enemy's playbook is limited but effective when unrecognized. Some of his most common schemes include:

1. Offense — Using words, actions, or misunderstandings to produce bitterness. (Matthew 24:10–12)
2. Lies and Accusations — The enemy is called "the accuser of the brethren" (Revelation 12:10). He whispers condemnation and suspicion.

3. Fear and Intimidation — He paralyzes with "what ifs" and imaginations (2 Timothy 1:7).
4. Sickness and Infirmity — Jesus often bound spirits of infirmity before healing (Luke 13:11–12).
5. False Reports and Confusion — As Nehemiah experienced, enemies spread lies to weaken builders (Nehemiah 6:8–9).

If you don't discern these as spiritual tactics, you will fight people, blame yourself, or give up. But when you discern them, you can bind them and loose Heaven's opposite reality.

My Experience With Misplaced Battle

For years, I misdirected my battle. Professors at Bible college slandered me, a boss at the cell tower company lied about me — and I thought they were the enemy. I fought them in my heart with bitterness, replaying conversations, wasting energy in offense. But those were never the real enemies. They were people under influence, sometimes knowingly, sometimes not. The true battle was spiritual. The enemy was sowing lies, stirring jealousy, and trying to bait me into unforgiveness.

Had I discerned correctly, I would have bound the spirit of accusation and loosed truth. I would have bound strife and loosed peace. Instead, I carried burdens I was never meant to carry. This is why discernment is vital. Without it, we fight people. With it, we fight powers.

Jesus' Example of Discernment

Jesus constantly demonstrated discernment. When Peter tried to talk Him out of going to the cross, Jesus did not fight Peter. He said:

"Get behind Me, Satan! You are an offense to Me, for you are not mindful of the things of God, but the things of men." (Matthew 16:23) NKJV

He discerned the voice behind the words. Peter loved Jesus, but Satan was attempting to influence him. Jesus bound the spirit's influence in that moment, even while continuing to disciple and love Peter. That is maturity: discerning the spirit without discarding the person.

Resisting the Devil

James 4:7 gives the clearest instruction:

"Therefore submit to God. Resist the devil and he will flee from you." NKJV

Resisting is not passive. It is active refusal. To resist is to bind what Heaven forbids. And notice the order: first submit to God. Authority flows from alignment. When we are aligned with God's will, our resistance carries weight. Resisting the devil in daily life looks like this:

- When fear whispers, bind it and loose peace.
- When lies accuse, bind them and loose truth.
- When offense tempts, bind bitterness and loose forgiveness.
- When sickness strikes, bind infirmity and loose healing.

Resistance is not complicated, but it must be consistent.

Reflection: Am I Fighting People?

Ask yourself:

- Am I spending more energy resenting people than resisting spirits?
- Am I discerning the real scheme, or am I distracted by surface conflict?
- Am I quick to forgive people while binding the powers behind their actions?

Sample Prayers of Discernment and Resistance

Over Offense:

Father, I bind the spirit of offense, bitterness, and unforgiveness. I loose love, grace, and mercy into my heart. I release those who wronged me, and I align with Your truth.

Over Fear:

In Jesus' name, I bind the spirit of fear and intimidation. I loose peace, courage, and the mind of Christ. I declare I have not received a spirit of fear, but of power, love, and a sound mind.

Over False Accusation:

I bind every lie and accusation spoken against me. I loose truth, vindication, and favor. I declare that no weapon formed against me shall prosper, and every tongue that rises against me in judgment I condemn, for this is my heritage as a servant of the Lord.

Activation Prayer

Pray this aloud:

Father, thank You for opening my eyes to discern the schemes of the enemy. I declare today that I will not waste energy fighting people. I forgive those who have wronged me. I bind the powers of darkness influencing them and loose Your truth, peace, and freedom. I put on the whole armor of God and stand firm against the wiles of the devil. I resist fear, lies, and offense. I loose life, truth, and abundance in every area of my life. In Jesus' name, amen.

Discerning and resisting the enemy is a core part of binding and loosing. Without discernment, we fight people and lose battles. With discernment, we identify the true adversary and exercise authority effectively.

Remember: the thief only comes to steal, kill, and destroy — but Jesus has come to give life. Binding and loosing is how sons and daughters enforce that abundant life.

Do not waste another day shadowboxing people. Take your stand, resist the devil, and watch him flee.

6

THE POWER OF DECREES AND PROPHETIC AGREEMENT

LIFE AND DEATH IN THE TONGUE

THE BOOK OF PROVERBS MAKES A STAGGERING CLAIM:

"Death and life are in the power of the tongue, and those who love it will eat its fruit." (Proverbs 18:21, NKJV)

Words carry power. They are not mere sounds or sentiments. They are spiritual seeds, either carrying life or releasing death. Every conversation, prayer, and declaration is either reinforcing Heaven's reality or empowering hell's agenda.

Binding and loosing finds its greatest expression in this truth. To bind is to forbid with words; to loose is to permit with words. Authority is exercised not silently in our thoughts, but vocally through our decrees. This is why Jesus Himself demonstrated authority by speaking. He rebuked storms with words. He cast out demons with commands. He healed the sick by declaring freedom. Words, spoken in alignment with Heaven, carried creative, destructive, and legislative power.

The Power of a Decree

Job 22:28 declares:

"You will also declare a thing, and it will be established for you; so light will shine on your ways." NKJV

A decree is more than a prayer request. It is the authoritative declaration of God's will into the earth. When you decree what Heaven has already spoken, it becomes established. Light shines. Darkness flees. Order replaces chaos. Isaiah 55:11 reinforces this:

"So shall My word be that goes forth from My mouth; it shall not return to Me void, but it shall accomplish what I please, and it shall prosper in the thing for which I sent it." NKJV

God's Word never returns empty. When you loose His Word by declaring it, it does not evaporate into thin air. It carries divine assignment until it accomplishes its purpose.

Waging Warfare With Prophecy

Paul exhorted Timothy:

"This charge I commit to you, son Timothy, according to the prophecies previously made concerning you, that by them you may wage the good warfare." (1 Timothy 1:18) NKJV

Prophetic words are not meant to be admired like souvenirs. They are weapons. To wage warfare with prophecy is to decree what God has spoken until it manifests.

When a prophetic word declares that your children will walk with the Lord, you bind rebellion and loose destiny with your decrees. When a prophecy confirms business expansion, you bind financial blockages and loose divine provision. When a prophetic promise declares healing, you bind sickness and loose restoration. Prophecy is Heaven's blueprint; decrees are how we build it on earth.

Defensive vs. Offensive Decrees

There are two main ways decrees function:

<u>1. Defensive Decrees (Resisting Attacks)</u>

- Binding sickness, loosing healing.
- Binding fear, loosing peace.
- Binding strife, loosing unity.

These are like shields that guard what God has already entrusted to you.

<u>2. Offensive Decrees (Advancing Destiny)</u>

- Declaring prophetic words into reality.
- Speaking new assignments into being.
- Calling forth expansion, influence, and breakthrough.

These are like battering rams that open new territory. Both are necessary. Without defensive decrees, you lose ground. Without offensive decrees, you fail to advance. Mature sons and daughters do both.

Example: Decreeing Destiny Over My Children

When doctors said my wife could not carry children, I refused to accept their decree. I spoke the opposite. I declared that God opens and closes the womb, that children are a heritage from the Lord, and that His promises stand above medical limitations.

Later, when Ezra was born and doctors claimed he had a fused skull that would require surgery, I decreed the opposite. I declared there was nothing wrong with my son. I spoke life, health, and wholeness over him. The CAT scan confirmed what Heaven already said — there was no issue. That same day, as I prayed, the swelling on his head disappeared under my hand.

These were decrees — not wishes. They were spoken declarations aligned with Heaven's truth, resisting the enemy's lies, and loosing God's will into the earth.

Agreement Multiplies Authority

Jesus emphasized the power of agreement in Matthew 18:19–20:

"Again I say to you that if two of you agree on earth concerning anything that they ask, it will be done for them by My Father in heaven. For where two or three are gathered together in My name, I am there in the midst of them." NKJV

Agreement multiplies decrees. One voice carries authority; two or more in unity amplify it. Hell trembles not just at lone soldiers, but at united armies. This is why families should decree together. Churches should decree corporately. Teams should bind and loose in unity. Agreement not only multiplies authority, it draws the manifest presence of Jesus.

How to Form Effective Decrees

1. Anchor in Scripture — Always start with what God has already said. Decree His Word, not your feelings.
2. Align With Prophecy — Recall prophetic words you've received and declare them. They are blueprints waiting for enforcement.
3. Speak With Authority — Don't ask timidly; decree boldly. Sons legislate, they don't beg.
4. Stay Consistent — Decrees are not "one and done." They are daily enforcement until Heaven's reality manifests.
5. Combine With Binding — Bind the opposite spirit while loosing the decree. (Example: Bind poverty, loose provision.)

Examples of Prophetic Decrees

Over Family:

"I decree that my household shall serve the Lord. I bind rebellion, deception, and confusion. I loose salvation, unity, and the Spirit of wisdom over my children."

Over Finances:

"I decree that my God supplies all my needs according to His

riches in glory. I bind lack, theft, and dishonesty. I loose favor,
integrity, and abundance in my work."

Over Health:

"I decree that by the stripes of Jesus, I am healed. I bind sickness,
diagnosis, and fear. I loose life, wholeness, and strength into my
body."

Over Destiny:

"I decree that every prophetic word spoken over my life will come
to pass. I bind delay, distraction, and intimidation. I loose
acceleration, boldness, and breakthrough into my calling."

Reflection Questions

- Am I merely reacting to attacks, or am I proactively decreeing God's will?
- Do I know the prophetic words spoken over my life, and am I waging warfare with them?
- Am I speaking more of my fears, or more of God's promises?
- Who do I need to partner with in agreement to multiply authority in this season?

Activation Prayer

Pray this aloud today:

Father, thank You for the power of decrees. Thank You that my
words, aligned with Yours, establish Your will on earth. Today, I
bind lies, fear, and delay. I loose truth, faith, and breakthrough. I

decree that every promise You have spoken over my life, my family, and my calling will come to pass. I decree health, provision, unity, and destiny. I join my agreement with Heaven and with others who stand in faith, and I declare that Your Word will not return void. In Jesus' name, amen.

Binding and loosing is not only defensive — it is creative and prophetic. With decrees, sons and daughters release Heaven into the earth. With agreement, they multiply authority and invite Jesus' presence.

Every decree aligned with Heaven establishes His will and dismantles the enemy's schemes. This is the privilege of sons: not to wait for the future, but to legislate the present.

7

WALKING OUT KINGDOM AUTHORITY AS A SON

AUTHORITY AS LIFESTYLE, NOT EVENT

MANY CHRISTIANS TREAT SPIRITUAL AUTHORITY LIKE A FIRE extinguisher — something you grab only in emergencies. But Jesus intended it to be more like oxygen — something you breathe every day. Sons and daughters don't "use authority" occasionally; they walk in it continually. Binding and loosing is not a ritual for crises; it is the rhythm of a son. You are not a servant reacting to chaos, you are a son stewarding order. You are not a victim managing attacks, you are a priest and king legislating Heaven's will.

This chapter shows what it looks like to walk in Kingdom authority as a son — in prayer, in daily life, and in advancing assignments.

The Lord's Prayer: A Son's Blueprint

Jesus gave us the clearest framework in Matthew 6:9–13, often called The Lord's Prayer. Many treat it as a memorized ritual, but it is a divine blueprint for walking out authority.

"In this manner, therefore, pray: Our Father in heaven, Hallowed be Your name. Your kingdom come. Your will be done on earth as it is in heaven. Give us this day our daily bread. And forgive us our debts, as we forgive our debtors. And do not lead us into temptation, but deliver us from the evil one. For Yours is the kingdom and the power and the glory forever. Amen." NKJV

Break it down, and you see the rhythm of a son stewarding authority:

- Identity and Worship: Our Father — you begin as a son, not a beggar. Authority flows from intimacy.
- Binding and Loosing: Your kingdom come, Your will be done — this is the daily rhythm of forbidding what Heaven forbids and releasing what Heaven allows.
- Provision: Give us this day our daily bread — loosing Heaven's supply, wisdom, and creativity.
- Forgiveness: Forgive us… as we forgive — binding unforgiveness, loosing mercy.
- Protection: Deliver us from the evil one — binding temptation, loosing deliverance and victory.
- Governance: For Yours is the kingdom, the power, and the glory — declaring whose authority ultimately rules.

This prayer is not a formula to recite but a daily pattern to live.

Sons Steward Atmospheres

Sons are called to carry the government of God on their shoulders (Isaiah 9:6). That government is not abstract; it applies to every atmosphere you step into:

- Home: binding strife, loosing peace.
- Marriage: binding division, loosing covenant love.
- Children: binding rebellion, loosing destiny.
- Workplace: binding dishonesty, loosing integrity.
- Community: binding injustice, loosing righteousness.
- Church: binding confusion, loosing unity.

Every atmosphere you touch reveals whether you live as a son stewarding order or as a servant reacting to chaos. Sons take responsibility; they don't shrug it off.

Three Rhythms of Authority

Walking as a son requires three ongoing rhythms:

1. Daily Prayers (Covering)

Every morning, sons and daughters use the keys to set the tone for the day. This is not paranoia; it is governance. Just as Adam was told to "tend and keep" the garden (Genesis 2:15), you must tend and keep the garden of your life daily. Examples:

- Bind fear, loose peace.
- Bind distraction, loose focus.
- Bind anxiety, loose joy.

2. Defensive Warfare (Resisting)

When attacks come, sons resist actively, not passively. James 4:7 says, "Submit to God. Resist the devil and he will flee from you."Examples:

- When false accusations arise, bind lies and loose truth.
- When sickness strikes, bind infirmity and loose healing.
- When offense tempts, bind bitterness and loose forgiveness.

3. Advancing Declarations (Offensive)

Sons don't just defend; they build. They enforce prophetic words with decrees. They declare new seasons into existence. They loose Heaven's future into the present. Examples:

- Declaring your household will serve the Lord.
- Prophesying business expansion aligned with God's will.
- Decreeing revival over your city.

Walking With God's Voice

Authority is not mechanical. It flows from intimacy. Jesus said in John 10:27:

"My sheep hear My voice, and I know them, and they follow Me." NKJV

Hearing His voice is essential for binding and loosing. Without His Word and Spirit, decrees are empty. But when aligned with His voice, decrees carry Heaven's weight. A son hears the Father's voice and declares it. Jesus modeled this in John 5:19:

> *"Most assuredly, I say to you, the Son can do nothing of Himself, but what He sees the Father do; for whatever He does, the Son also does in like manner." NKJV*

Authority flows from revelation. Sons legislate what the Father reveals.

From Theory to Practice

Walking in Kingdom authority is not theory; it is practice. Here are practical steps to cultivate it:

1. Start Your Day in Authority — Before engaging emails, news, or tasks, bind and loose. Set the atmosphere.
2. Discern Throughout the Day — When tension arises, ask: Is this just circumstance, or is there a spirit behind it? Bind accordingly.
3. End Your Day With Decrees — Declare over your family, assignment, and future before you sleep.
4. Agree With Others — Partner in prayer. Agreement multiplies authority.
5. Track Fulfillment — Write down decrees and prophetic promises. Journal how God fulfills them.

My Journey of Growing Into Sonship

When I didn't understand sonship, I lived constantly reacting — offended at professors, hurt by bosses, frustrated by circumstances. But when I began to see myself as a son and priest with keys in my hand, I stopped reacting and started governing.

Instead of praying timid prayers, I began to declare: "This will not stand. This is not Heaven's will." I saw environments shift, battles won, and prophetic words fulfilled. The difference was not just knowledge, but identity. I wasn't just Tom, struggling believer — I was a son, a king, and a priest enforcing the Father's will.

Reflection Questions

- Am I living like a son stewarding atmospheres, or a servant reacting to chaos?
- Do I use authority daily, or only in emergencies?
- Am I walking in all three rhythms: daily covering, defensive warfare, and advancing decrees?
- Am I aligning with God's voice and Word, or declaring my own desires?

Activation Prayer

Pray this aloud:

Father, thank You for calling me a son and entrusting me with the keys of the Kingdom. Today I step into my role as a priest and king. I bind fear, strife, and every scheme of the enemy. I loose peace, love, and truth into my life, family, and assignment. I declare that I will not react as a servant but govern as a son. I choose daily covering, defensive resistance, and advancing decrees. I align with Your voice and release Your will on earth as it is in Heaven. In Jesus' name, amen.

Walking out Kingdom authority as a son means binding and loosing as both rhythm and weapon. You guard what God has entrusted daily, you resist attacks decisively, and you advance into new territory boldly. This is the lifestyle Jesus envisioned when He placed the keys of the Kingdom into our hands. Not a powerless waiting, but a governing partnership. Not a servant's fear, but a son's confidence.

Everywhere you go, atmospheres shift, strongholds break, and Heaven's will manifests — because you are walking as a son carrying the government of God on your shoulders.

CONCLUSION

BUILDERS OF THE FATHER'S HOUSE

Isaiah's prophecy still echoes across eternity:

"For unto us a Child is born, unto us a Son is given; and the government will be upon His shoulder. And His name will be called Wonderful, Counselor, Mighty God, Everlasting Father, Prince of Peace. Of the increase of His government and peace there will be no end..." (Isaiah 9:6–7, NKJV)

The government of God rests not on angels, not on institutions, but upon the shoulders of sons. Christ the Son has carried it perfectly, and now He entrusts it to His body — sons and daughters who walk in His name and legislate His will on earth.

When you bind what Heaven forbids, you shoulder His government. When you loose what Heaven permits, you shoulder His government. When you stand in prayer over your family, workplace, church, or city, you are literally carrying the government of the King into that sphere.

The Eternal Plan of God

Paul captures the big picture in Ephesians 1:9–10:

"Having made known to us the mystery of His will, according to His good pleasure which He purposed in Himself, that in the dispensation of the fullness of the times He might gather together in one all things in Christ, both which are in heaven and which are on earth—in Him." NKJV

God's ultimate plan is to reunite Heaven and earth under Christ's headship. Binding and loosing is not just about solving personal problems — it is about partnering with that eternal plan. Every time you forbid hell's agenda and release Heaven's will, you are participating in God's cosmic restoration project. You are not simply "getting through life" until Heaven. You are part of Heaven invading earth.

Stop Waiting, Start Governing

Far too many believers live as though the Christian life is simply surviving until Heaven. But Jesus never taught His disciples to wait passively. He taught them to pray actively:

"Your Kingdom come. Your will be done on earth as it is in Heaven." NKJV

Sons don't wait for permission; they walk in assignment. Sons don't retreat from opposition; they advance through it. Sons don't cower in fear; they bind fear and loose courage. This is your invitation: to step out of passive Christianity and into governing sonship.

Your Sphere of Government

God has entrusted you with atmospheres — your home, your relationships, your work, your church, and your city. Those are not random environments; they are spheres of government.

- In your home, bind strife, loose peace.
- In your marriage, bind division, loose covenant love.
- Over your children, bind rebellion, loose destiny.
- In your workplace, bind corruption, loose integrity.
- In your city, bind injustice, loose righteousness.

Every son and daughter has been given territory. The question is not whether you have authority — Jesus already gave you the keys. The question is whether you will use them.

The Call to Builders

The Hebrew word ben — son — means "builder of the father's house." That is your calling. Sons don't just receive inheritance; they build legacy. Sons don't just live blessed; they establish environments where others can flourish. Binding and loosing is not only for you; it is for those who will come after you. When you govern atmospheres today, you shape the inheritance for your children and spiritual sons and daughters tomorrow. You are a builder of the Father's house, and that house is expanding.

A Commissioning Challenge

As you close this book, you stand at a threshold. The keys of the Kingdom are in your hand. The Father is inviting you to stop waiting and start governing.

- Will you bind what is illegal in Heaven so it no longer operates in your sphere?
- Will you loose what is permissible in Heaven so that it manifests in your home, church, and city?
- Will you stop shadowboxing with people and start legislating against principalities?
- Will you walk daily as a son, not occasionally as a servant?

This is not a teaching to admire; it is a lifestyle to embrace.

Commissioning Prayer

Pray this aloud as your commissioning:

Father, I thank You that I am a son in Your house, a priest and king in Your Kingdom. I thank You for entrusting me with the keys of binding and loosing. Today I step into my authority with boldness. I bind fear, sickness, strife, confusion, and every work of the enemy in my life and in the territories You have entrusted to me. I loose peace, health, love, wisdom, provision, and unity. I decree that my household will serve the Lord. I declare that my city will experience revival. I proclaim that Heaven's government is advancing through me. I stop waiting and start governing. I embrace my role as a builder of the Father's house, carrying His government on my shoulders. In Jesus' name, amen.

Final Word

The forgotten key has been placed in your hands. What will you do with it? Sons and daughters were never meant to live powerless, waiting for Heaven someday. You were created to legislate Heaven today. Bind what is illegal. Loose what is divine. Govern as a son. Build as a priest. Reign as a king. And as you do, the increase of His government and peace will know no end.

APPENDIX A

BONUS SECTION — BINDING
AND LOOSING PRAYER MANUAL

How to Use This Manual

This prayer guide is not a formula — it is a framework. Every prayer of binding and loosing must flow from intimacy with the Father and agreement with His Word. Pray these aloud with faith, and then add your own decrees as the Spirit leads. Remember:

- Bind = forbid what Heaven forbids.
- Loose = release what Heaven permits.
- Always align with God's Word.
- Always decree from your identity as a son or daughter.

Workplace & Finances

<u>Bind:</u> strife, dishonesty, poverty, intimidation, fear of man.
<u>Loose:</u> favor, integrity, wisdom, abundance, divine creativity.

Sample Prayers:

- *"In Jesus' name, I bind every spirit of strife, gossip, and dishonesty in my workplace. I forbid fear and intimidation from operating against me. I loose favor with my supervisors, integrity in my work, and abundance through the labor of my hands."*
- *"I bind the spirit of poverty and lack that seeks to devour my finances. I loose provision, wisdom in stewardship, and supernatural creativity to generate wealth for Kingdom purposes."*
- *"Father, I decree that my workplace will not be an atmosphere of stress and division but of excellence, innovation, and peace."*

Marriage & Family

<u>Bind:</u> division, confusion, generational curses, unforgiveness, manipulation.
<u>Loose:</u> covenant love, unity, communication, blessing, generational legacy.

Sample Prayers:

- *"In Jesus' name, I bind division, confusion, and unforgiveness in my marriage. I forbid manipulation and dishonor from taking root. I loose covenant love, unity of heart and mind, and joy in our relationship."*
- *"I bind every generational curse of brokenness, divorce, or abuse. I loose generational blessing, faithfulness, and a legacy of love and honor that will flow to my children and grandchildren."*
- *"Father, I decree that my household shall reflect Christ and His Church — filled with sacrificial love, mutual honor, and the blessing of Your presence."*

Children & Legacy

<u>Bind:</u> rebellion, deception, premature death, confusion about identity.
<u>Loose:</u> wisdom, destiny, protection, purity, boldness in faith.

Sample Prayers:

- *"In Jesus' name, I bind every spirit of rebellion, deception, and premature death assigned against my children. I forbid confusion about their identity from taking root. I loose wisdom, purity, protection, and clarity of purpose over their lives."*
- *"I bind every generational assignment of addiction, perversion, and fear. I loose boldness in faith, godly friendships, and the fire of the Holy Spirit upon my sons and daughters."*
- *"Father, I decree that my children will fulfill their prophetic destiny, walk in integrity, and rise as leaders for Your Kingdom."*

Health & Healing

<u>Bind:</u> sickness, fear, false diagnoses, premature death, anxiety.
<u>Loose:</u> divine health, healing, peace, strength, longevity.

Sample Prayers:

- *"In Jesus' name, I bind sickness, disease, and every lying diagnosis that contradicts God's Word. I loose healing, life, and restoration into my body and my household."*

- *"I bind fear and anxiety that attach to medical reports. I loose peace of mind, strength for today, and faith in God's promises."*
- *"Father, I decree that my body is the temple of the Holy Spirit. I bind premature death and loose longevity and wholeness to glorify You."*

Community & Nation

<u>Bind:</u> corruption, injustice, violence, demonic agendas.
<u>Loose:</u> righteousness, peace, revival, godly leadership, truth.

Sample Prayers:

- *"In Jesus' name, I bind corruption, injustice, and violence in my city and nation. I forbid demonic agendas from advancing in government, schools, and culture."*
- *"I loose righteousness, truth, and justice into every level of leadership. I call forth godly leaders, revival fire, and a return to the fear of the Lord."*
- *"Father, I decree that my city will be known not for darkness but for the light of revival, unity, and transformation."*

Personal Identity & Destiny

<u>Bind:</u> shame, fear, orphan spirit, doubt, passivity.
<u>Loose:</u> sonship, confidence, boldness, peace, Kingdom purpose.

Sample Prayers:

- *"In Jesus' name, I bind shame, fear, and every orphan mindset. I forbid lies that say I am unwanted, powerless, or unworthy. I loose my true identity as a son of God, seated with Christ in heavenly places."*
- *"I bind timidity and doubt, and I loose boldness, confidence, and the spirit of adoption that cries out, 'Abba, Father.'"*
- *"Father, I decree that I will walk in my Kingdom purpose, advancing Your will in every sphere You've entrusted to me."*

Create Your Own Decrees

Use this format:

- "I bind [specific spirit/attack]. I forbid it from operating in my life/family/workplace."
- "I loose [specific blessing/promise]. I release Heaven's will into this situation."

Write your own prayers here:

Closing Commissioning Prayer

Father, thank You for entrusting me with the keys of the Kingdom. Today I choose to use them with boldness. I bind every scheme of the enemy and forbid darkness from ruling in my life, family, and city. I loose Heaven's will — peace, healing, provision, unity, revival, and destiny. I declare that I am a son, a priest, and a king. I will no longer wait passively but legislate actively. Let Your Kingdom come and Your will be done, in me and through me, on earth as it is in Heaven. In Jesus' name, amen.

APPENDIX B

Daily Binding & Loosing Routine

(Pray this aloud each morning as a son/daughter with Kingdom authority.)

1. Identity Declaration

"Father, I thank You that I am Your child, a priest and king in Your Kingdom. Today I rise in my identity, seated with Christ in heavenly places. I choose to walk in Your authority and release Heaven on earth."

2. Personal Life

- I bind fear, shame, and every orphan mindset.
- I loose sonship, peace, joy, and boldness in Christ.

3. Family & Marriage

- I bind division, confusion, and generational curses.
- I loose covenant love, unity, blessing, and generational legacy.

4. Children & Legacy

- I bind rebellion, deception, and premature death.
- I loose wisdom, protection, purity, and prophetic destiny over my children and spiritual sons/daughters.

5. Health & Body

- I bind sickness, infirmity, and anxiety.
- I loose divine health, healing, strength, and longevity.

6. Work & Finances

- I bind strife, dishonesty, lack, and intimidation.
- I loose favor, integrity, creativity, and abundance for Kingdom purposes.

7. Community & Nation

- I bind corruption, violence, and demonic agendas.
- I loose righteousness, revival, godly leadership, and truth in my city and nation.

8. Advancing Declarations

"I decree that I will fulfill my prophetic destiny. I declare that doors of favor and influence are opening before me. I loose acceleration and breakthrough for every assignment God has placed in my hands. No weapon formed against me shall prosper."

Closing Commissioning

"Father, I carry Your government on my shoulders as Your son. I bind what is illegal in Heaven and forbid it from operating here. I loose what is established in Heaven and release it into earth. Today, I walk in Kingdom authority — not as a victim, but as a son and builder of Your house. In Jesus' name, amen."

ABOUT THE AUTHOR

Tom Cornell is the Senior Leader of SOZO Church in Washington state, founder of Walk in the Light International and SOZO Network. Tom is married to his beautiful wife Katy and lives in the Puget Sound area with her and their three kids. He has been in ministry pastoring and teaching the body of Christ since 2008.

He has a passion to see the body of Christ moving from people with an orphan mindset to that of sonship; equipping the body to do the work of Jesus resulting in seeing the Kingdom of God manifested here on earth.